Preferential Psychology

By Dr Mona Aeysha Khalid

Acknowledgement

I am grateful to the Universe, who has provided me with the wisdom to write on this topic.

Thanks Load

TABLE OF CONTENTS

CHAPTER1: INTRODUCTION

This book is about your attitude for preferring someone, something, or some concept in any particular time. You will come to know about the different categories of the preferences and about their true nature. You will also comprehend about the possible preferential mistakes that you are used to perform, unconsciously in your day to day life.

When you are fully aware of your preferences in detail, you are unlikely to make any further judgement error. You will no more regret for your wrong decisions and repent on your wasted energy, time and money on useless choices.

To change our preferences according to our needs is the most important tool to survive and become successful. This book deals with such issues in detail and we come to know the strategy to change our mind-set and decide better in right time.

Preferences in this book stand for our 'choices', likes', 'dislikes', and attitude to select something and ignore something else at a particular time to fulfil our needs and become happy. We go through a long process of decision making while preferring something; however decision making techniques are out of the scope of this book. Hope the readers will enjoy the book as well as learn something new.

Thanks

CHAPTER 2: WHAT IS YOUR FAVOURAITE COLOR?

Preference psychology is based on our instinct of comparison and it emerges since birth, but we are hardly aware of it as it stays in our unconscious level. With maturity, our skills and thoughts take shape until we learn to analyze properly in adulthood. It is a highly organized procedure as we continue comparing things in a unique way and develop certain thinking styles/attitudes at the end.

Here my focus is not on ' comparison processes' or how these skills are developed rather on 'preferences' that we keep without knowing their origin or structural characteristics. These preferences are analyzed via instruments in thousands of research processes mentioned in the psychology books and journal articles, to get a full access of human psychology and even to understand our own self fully. Indeed, our overall psychology is based on these preferences. For example, questionnaires on self-esteem, self-concept, personality disorders, attitudes, happiness, learning, memory, intelligence, and emotions. Almost all aspects of psychology use preferences by categorizing them for a specific reason to induce reliable results.

By nature, preferences are simply the 'choices', likes and dislikes made in a specific environment based on similar experiences. For example, a person has developed a preference for the color-blue in his 40's. His preference might be based on many experiences in life which make him believe that blue is lucky for him or it is the color that suits him. Quoting another example in this regard, a person 'a' said, "When I was a child, I used to like red because I had lots of red cars. When I grew up, I started fascinating black as I heard decent boys would dress up in black. When I reached my young age, I started liking brown as I came to know that brown color was a symbol of our intellect, elegance and sobriety. When I entered in my early adulthood, I slightly changed my mind and started liking light colors as this was the trend at that time. When I passed my 40's I analyzed my choice of color thoroughly and established different color preferences for different items. For instance: black for cars, white for paint, silver for home decoration, gold for jewelry items, brown for furniture, light colors for clothing, etc. Now if you ask me what my favorite color is, it sounds a little odd/vague and incomplete question to me. Moreover, I cannot say what exactly will be my choice in old age! ".

From the above example, we can well understand that preference of color is going to change as a result of a change in time, age, knowledge (about colors), experiences, beliefs, mood, and many other social factors. Moreover, when we are asked what our favorite color is, we are not provided with full range of colors including all shades to decide about our favorite one. On the other side, we could not choose the right color due to having lots of choices available at a time. Sometimes we are not aware of the psyche of colors properly that if we knew, our choice would have been slightly different or all together changed.

If we are mature and able to analyze more, we will need more information to understand even our own preferred color. For example, choosing colors for what use, for what event, for which dress type, and in what context. After having answers to all of such questions, we will be able to better understand our true preference for the color. In this example, the word 'color' stands for the choice we make in our life for any phenomenon. Therefore, like colors we all have many kinds of preferences in our lives that all depend upon our understanding of such phenomenon in the light of experiences, beliefs, social and cultural norms, knowledge, religious and ethical factors and our own interpretation and reflection.

To further elaborate the concept, preferences are divided into different categories in the following chapter.

CHAPTER 3: BASIC CATEGORIES OF PREFERENCES

Preferences are choices and we start making choices since the day we are born. In childhood, we had a choice to drink milk or water, to play with toys or go outside, and to watch television or go to bed. Then we expand our range of choices and keep on making such choices in life until death. There are thousand ways to solve our problems in the world of psychology. However, our understanding of our preferences would play an important role in solving some of them.

Preferences are not static   rather they are continuous and part of our development. They would change with many conscious or unconscious happenings around us or inside us.

We can divide preferences into ten different categories:

1. Instant Preferences

When we need to select something in no time, we prefer something to another. For example: something bought in a market in a hurry, some membership signed up hurriedly, or any decision taken place without much evaluation or time spent to see pros and cons.

2. Preferences based on concepts

When we learn different concepts about life, religion, morality and ethics, we do follow them blindly and set some sort of preference accordingly. For example: a person claims that he is a religious being, he would follow the paths he thinks are religious. Then a person thinks he should prefer his career to his love. He might leave his love for his big career in the future.

3. Preferences based on experiences

When we get rewarded in response to our performance, we prefer to do that activity again. When we do fail in something, we tend to avoid such activity in the future or try it again reluctantly. We may not like it so much in the future.

4. Preferences based on other's preferences

When we love someone, we tend to follow his or her preferences consciously or unconsciously. For example: some students blindly follow their teachers' preferences in life because they love them so much. Couples who love each other, not only respect each other's preferences, rather adapt to them.

5. Preferences based on needs

When we need something in real, we just prefer that thing. For example: a girl needs a warm sweater in winter. Although she would prefer a lightweight and small one to wear in ordinary circumstances, but now she chooses a long, heavy and thick one because that would satisfy her present needs. Take another example: If you are thirsty, and in need of a glass of water, you will not buy any other drink. That drink you may prefer to buy in a normal situation.

6. Preferences based on social pressure

Sometimes we prefer something just to satisfy our parents, friends, relatives, or other significant people around us. For example: People living in underdeveloped countries, prefer to live in London than living in their home town due to the reason they have a social pressure to live abroad in any case. Their relatives and parents feel pride that their beloved is living in London (a better place). Similarly, someone going to study medicine to fulfil his parents wish, is another example. Say, you are taking a course on the wish of your friends. There could be several other examples to quote in this regard.

7. Preferences based on limited alternatives

When we have no choice or limited choices available, we can very easily set our criteria. For example: a person has only two choices available to pass his leisure time - either sit in front of television or go for a walk. He goes for a walk and loves that. Although he says that he prefers 'walking' to other activities, yet in reality he has not many choices to choose from. Take another example: you have only two options to work. Either go, for business online or share with someone to buy a shop. You select the one that suits you. Here your preference is only based on your limited opportunities.

8. Preferences based on age factors

Sometimes we prefer something because of our developmental changes. A child may prefer a bright color to wear. A teenager would love to wear the fashion colors. The same person in his adulthood may find it inappropriate and would choose more sober-colors. Take another example: you buy toys suitable to your age level in your life. With the age, your preferred toys change and in your mature age, you would not buy any toy rather things of your interest. Your interest in different items will also depend on your maturity level. Same goes for other things.

9. Preferences based on our knowledge

Sometimes we simply are not aware of some products, food items, concepts in life, ways of life, thinking styles, and the nature of people around us. So we decide to prefer one to another due to our limited knowledge about things. For example: you go to market and buy something. A salesman encourages you to test his new product instead of the old one. For the first time, you will not feel comfortable in buying that product. After testing and liking it, you will change your mindset and prefer the new product to the old one in the future. The same is true for other matters of life.

10. Preferences based on other factors

Between two similar preferences, the stronger one will win based on other factors important to you at a particular time. Therefore, it is very important to keep track of such factors as they also help us in determining our true preferences. For example: a person is fond of snow and prefers living in a cold country to living in a hot region with the warm sunny weather all around the year. Whereas to spend summer vacations, he chooses Miami for a beach life. Thus his love of beach life would affect his preference for cold weather in a particular time frame. Take another example: a girl usually wears bright colors and shiny shoes in her daily life. Whereas to meet her friend in a funeral ceremony, she prefers a modest dress compared to her personal choice (the bright one). Have you ever noticed someone stating something else for his choice and doing something else?

So far you know about the basic categories of preferences that will serve as a background for the upcoming learning about the true nature of our preferences. Let's explore it!

CHAPTER 4: THE TRUE NATURE OF PREFERENCES

Preferences basically shape our lives, change our lifestyle, personality attributes and help in dealing with other constructs of psychology like decision making, emotional set backs, comparison processes, cognition, learning, and behavioral changes in many types of personality disorders. The true awareness of our preferences plays a significant role in achieving goals like to know ourselves better, to solve our problems, to become a better human being, to esteem us and others, and to take part actively/vigilantly in research activities.

To be fully aware of our preferences, we need to know the preferences of our family including father, mother and sibling preferences towards life; we need to know our society's, friends', and cultural preferences; we need to know the core beliefs about life we learn from the curriculum, teachers or significant others; we can study the preferences of people living in our region long time ago; moreover, we need to know our own childhood preferences that we can recollect from our memory or inquire about them from our teachers, parents or neighbors. Basically, these statements are important references to understand our preferences now and to change them in the future according to our needs and wishes.

Preferences based on certain concepts are irreplaceable, irresistible, and fundamental in nature, such as the concept of, right, wrong, good, bad, poor, rich, clean, dirty, beauty, ugliness, active, lazy, and a thousand others. It will not be wrong to say that the more concepts we learn in life, the more preferences we develop consciously or unconsciously. Especially preferences based on religious concepts are highly irreplaceable with detrimental attributes. Cultural beliefs are not less important, rather religious and cultural beliefs go side by side in some parts of the world. For example: In many parts of Pakistan and India, girls like long hairs due to beliefs like 'long hairs are good for girls', 'girls should not cut hairs', 'hairs are girls' honor' and 'girls' hair should not touch iron'. Thus, girls' preferences for hair styles in these regions are truly based on cultural as well as religious beliefs.

Preferences based on experiences 'good' or 'bad' provide us with a good example of classical conditioning. Though we can forget them through a process of extinction. If such experiences repeat for more than two or three times, we strongly support our preferences. For example: a man is scared to drive on a certain road because every time he drove there, he got some sort of accident or lost money. If the same person faces nothing bad on the same road, he will again change his mind for not preferring it anymore. He might prefer it in the future due to his recent experience (extinction). Let's take another example. A girl had a new hair cut, got much admiration from family and friends. The next time, she repeated the same hair cut and was again much appreciated by others. Now she admits that the hairstyle suits her very much and she prefers short hairs. Thus, there is always an obvious reason behind our preferences that could be from any trivial complement to a series of experiences.

Preferences based on limited exposure or due to having few alternatives in life cannot be fully justified. For example: a man likes to eat bread and eggs at breakfast and rice at lunch. When I asked how many types of breakfast, he had already experienced, he said the one or two. So his preference of bread is basically due to limited exposure of breakfasts/alternatives. It is one of the possibilities that after trying cereals, he would like or prefer cereals to breed. In the similar way, the experience of happiness is limited to our exposure. For example: a man says, ' I enjoy a lot when I go for a movie, while he has no other means to enjoy. The same person might change his mind, if he is exposed to swimming pool, beach life, horse riding, golf or any other activity. Hence, the number of choices available to us may change our preference for the leisure time activity.

Often contradiction between two persons' preferences creates confusion and put them in trouble. For example, you prefer to have simple food and save money to travel, but your partner is the other way round. You will be confused and bothered about the relationship status between you and your partner, ignoring the fact that it is only the difference of preference not the personality or feelings. Take another example: you are going to the library to read a book while your friend is going to the cinema to watch a movie to enjoy. You both prefer different things to satisfy the same need. There are several other examples to quote in this regard

Thus, it is very important to recognize the true nature of our preferences as well as others attitude towards them. Being fully aware of our preferences, we can choose a right path, to achieve our goals and save ourselves from conflicts, contradictions and misperceptions. To further extend the concept, the following chapter will summarize all possible mistakes that we could commit in our daily life with respect to preferences.

CHAPTER 5: CAUSES FOR WRONG PREFRENCES

Our behavior is determined by the choice of available preferences at a particular time. It relates to deciding something, selecting something, thinking something and ignoring the counterparts at the same time. The more choices we have, the more difficult our decision is. The fewer no of choices we have, the lesser time our decision-making would consume. We are often prone to select from our available resources at a particular time. We feel depressed if we cannot achieve what we want from our available resources. Our satisfaction does not rely upon something special in the world, rather it depends on what we think are available to us to choose from.

Therefor to modify someones's behavior, resources can be manipulated and interpreted accordingly. To create a sense of dissatisfaction, more options need to be developed and to create a sense of achievement and success, less options should be introduced. Hence, the number of options, being a great cause for our wrong preferences, depends on many factors: our need, our nature, our circumstances, our limitations and our attitude.

Likewise, to feel happy we need to concentrate on only a few things otherwise we will be stuck/depressed. We can focus on a few feelings, events, and people at a time to get clarity, concentration and peace of mind. If we focus on only one item at a time, it will be good for our mental and physical health. Similarly, 'one problem at a time' would be the best approach to solve our problems. In this regard, we can make a preference chart and start working on the first preferred item of the day- whether it is to buy something or a goal to achieve or a problem to resolve.

We are coded to prefer the best option available to us by nature. Though sometimes we make wrong decisions and regret our preferences forever. In such cases, we need to analyze our mistakes for our better future choices. However, there could be several reasons for our wrong preferences:

- When there is no time to truly compare things.

- When we really are in need of something, so we leave our true choice.

- When we miss other options available to us.

- When we are forced to select something by our circumstances.

- When we have limited resources available to us at a particular time.

- When we are used to select something else instead of keeping a true preference.

- When we are under the influence of someone or some belief temporarily.

- When we ignore our natural desire and become selfish and go for the benefits associated with the wrong choice.

- When we are in love and emotionally decide about something- not rationally.

- When we are told about our preferences in a negative manner.

- When we are not very much confident in making our choice –feel guilty instead.

Therefore, we have lots of channels through which we make wrong choices. We sometimes regret for our untimely or childish decisions for the whole of the life. Plus sometimes we continue choosing the wrong things for us. After a proper analysis of our wrong decisions, we can help ourselves not to repeat those mistakes in the future. This analysis will serve as a prevention against the guilt, regret, self condemnation, repentance, anguish, sorrow, pity, grief, depression, anxiety, and other sorts of diseases emerged from shocking decisions out-breaks of life. How can we do this? Please go ahead and see. The next chapter deals with how can we successfully change our preferences.

CHAPTER 6: HOW CAN WE CHANGE OUR PREFERENCES?

Preferences are continuously changing and shaping all the time unconsciously; however, we can change our 'preferences' consciously too, as they are always subject to change by nature. The only key is that we should be willing to change them. For example: a person wants to have a baby boy, not a baby girl and always seems gender biased in day to day activities. He needs to be educated that all human beings are respectful, equal in dignity and worth and no one is smaller to another in any capacity rather being meritorious (in goodness) should be the criteria- the only consideration if we have to prefer one to another. Similarly a woman who dislikes men due to her bitter experiences in life with men, may change her mind through counseling. She needs to understand that all men are not the same and she may find one good man for her in the future. She may recall some good experiences of her past with the men, good to her. In this way we can change our preferences and become less biased or neutral in our daily life.

We can change our pupils preferences of subjects too by giving them more information/knowledge, understanding and good experiences relating to those subjects they do not like. It is very obvious fact that children do like the subjects they know better and the subjects they find difficult to understand or with whom they have bad experiences in classroom learning, they do not like.

Sometimes to change our preference is a matter of life or death when we deal with life's most sensitive and delicate matters. For example: a person having no intimacy in his married life, feels depressed all the time, could not control his emotions, could not concentrate on anything and even decides to commit suicide. This problem needs to be solved otherwise the person would commit suicide one day. Here we will not go into the details of the actual matter: what is his job, nature, attitude, and what is his partners' job, nature, and attitude. Neither we will discuss his relationship-issues in detail. What we can do with reference to preferences, is to tell the person not to give preference to intimacy in life as much as he has already given. Intimacy plays an important role in married life, but it is not the all you need. It is not the core element/ ingredient or the basic thing to feel alive and successful. There are thousands of other issues to deal with, and to focus on, such as, hobbies, recreation plans, professional growth, social factors, health factors, and leisure attitude that if we pay attention to, we can enjoy our life fully. When he changes his frame of mind and develops a lesser degree of preference for intimacy, his half of the problem is solved. In addition to that, when he changes his attitude as well as develops other areas of life, his problem will be fully solved.

By having a real change in our life consciously or unconsciously, we can change our preferences. For example: a woman who is over caring and over loving and at the same time expects the same from her partner in the similar way. She is hurt and depressed easily with a single gesture of ignorance from her husband. She does so because she is overly dependent to her husband for money, communication, love, sex, care and for almost everything in life. She feels like she is from head to foot in love with her husband and she has no control over her feelings, and crazy attitudes. These are not the healthy signs of a happy married life. In this case husband is so proud that is taking advantage of his wife's total dependency on him and her poor nature. He often complaints her for not being caring, loving, and sexy in spite of her all efforts and struggles to please her husband to her level best. Bitter feelings among them continue until the time woman has a baby to look after. After having a child, she has got some other job (as a mother), some other identity (a mother), and another focus (a baby). Then she no more behaves like a crazy, mad and emotional woman who is in love with her husband only. Things settle down to some extent. Now she would not revolve around her husband all the time and would not expect a lot like before as she would also have something to do, more important than only loving her husband!

By exploring new beliefs to prefer, we feel protected, secure and content. For example: someone says, "I prefer being a poor man to a criminal". It is a set of choices someone chooses to protect his/her self-esteem as well as to save his/herself from anxieties emerged from poverty. Similarly, if someone prefers living alone to being with friends, he again is protecting his lonely feelings. It is very obvious that we intend to protect our concepts naturally and preferences are part of those very concepts developed through continuous and countless series of experiences.

By replacing one concept with another concept similar to the previous one. We can also change our attitude towards someone if we develop the same feelings for someone else. For example: a girl is facing break up stress with her recent boyfriend. She is in deep depression and anxiety. Although she can be advised to join some club, library, college, or something that interests her, to engage her in something else to heal and to become normal. However, if she finds a new friend to replace the old one, it will prove much easier and quicker fix for her troubles.

In short, if we are aware of the crux of our problems, we will be in a better place to find a solution to that otherwise we will be wandering alone and become despaired, psychotic and helpless. Similarly, if we know what our true preferences are, what preferences are causing trouble for us, what our preferences can or cannot be changed consciously, what preferences, we need to work on; we will definitely be able to control our life through a change in our preference psychology and be successful and happy in the end.

CHAPTER8: CONTRADICTORY PREFERENCES

When we live with someone we have to share many things from food to bed. In couples, usually arguments arise due to having a contradictory point of view about one object. Do you want to know what is the real truth about your partner with respect to love, sex and intimacy? Are you aware of your partner's true nature? Have you ever experienced your partner reacted differently somewhere beyond your expectations? If yes, then it is a case of contradictory preferences. Consider the following statements for a while:

- In normal circumstances, I would love to take you, but today I am more interested to go to university to see my friend.

- In normal circumstances, I would love to go to university to see my friend, but today I want to see my favorite movie last show in the cinema.

- In normal circumstances, I would love to go to the cinema to see that movie, but today I will have to arrange a job for my best friend.

- In normal circumstances, I would love to arrange a job for my best friend, but today my commitment with my son is more important.

- In normal circumstances, I would take my son to the park, but today I have to go for shopping first.

- In normal circumstances, I would go for the shopping first, but today I have to write a blog on my website.

- In normal circumstances, I would write a blog on my website, but today I am having a dinner outside.

In the above example, in each event, the preference is changed. The most preferred thing is our true nature that we just cannot postpone at any cost. We can also check our partner's preferences in different circumstances and finally evaluate which is his/her true preference.

We, for most of the time, think we know ourselves better, but it is not true. Whenever we have better options, we go for that. Whenever we have ailments and troubles, we leave our present state of preferences and think that health is our first priority. So we always compare our likes and dislikes with respect to their value that we assign. In other words, we would change our preferences if we have more alternatives. Therefore, preferences themselves are nothing; they should always be considered with respect to alternatives. For example: you have two choices available to choose from: red color or black color. You are bound to prefer one; otherwise your choice would have been different.

Some would argue in this regard that their preferences never change. In reality their likes and dislikes never change. Our behavior in terms of our actions is always based on our preferences. What we choose, we go for it, and that is our priority, likeness and selection at that time. Our preferences reflect our true nature. Others preferences reflect their true nature. Your preferences reflect your true nature. Yes, the preferences keep on changing, but they describe what you are - not you.

You cannot separate your preferences from time boundaries as well. Alternatives change with the time –so too preferences. Today you prefer Honda car and tomorrow you will be going to Toyota. Today you are having HP laptop and tomorrow you would prefer Toshiba. Thus, your preferences are strictly associated with the alternatives available at some specific time. Analyze them fully and your partner's to some extent and cool down. Your half of the problems must be resolved at this point. The rest ones should not take long if they are based on preferential contradictions.

CHAPTER 7: CONCLUSION

All our preferences cast a shadow on our lives partly or fully. It is a game for a young child to choose from different items and act accordingly. We have started preferring things since the day we are born. In the beginning our preferences are not very strong, rather flexible and changeable with little effort. With the passage of time, they take shape and the time comes when it is almost impossible to leave them. We love our preferences and stay with them whether they are right or wrong. However, when we encounter something wrong based on our preferences, we change our mind-set and create a new pathway in our brain. Thus we are continuously involved in a process of accommodation, and assimilation with respect to preferences.

The knowledge of our preferences can contribute a lot in eliminating pathways towards wrong decisions. When we know whom to prefer, and whom to ignore, we will never make judgment errors. When we know what is our true nature, what we need and what we like; we will never go for the wrong product, wrong belief, wrong choice. Right choice at the right time, will save us a lot of money, energy and time. We will never regret upon our wrong preferences-when we know what is preferential psychology.

To summarize, preferences are shaped as a result of experiences, conceptual information and several alternatives available to us at a particular time. They can easily be modified and changed further by extending alternatives, having new experiences, and through learning new concepts.

Thanks

About The Author:

Mona Aeysha Khalid, PhD, is an Educational and Developmental Psychologist, have been working as a Teacher, Counselor, and Researcher in several institutes of China, Pakistan and Cambodia.

Her major areas of interest are: self-esteem, self-concept, conceptual psychology, beliefs, self psychology, preferential psychology, cultural psychology and women psychology.

You are always welcome to contact her via email:

monaaeysha@gmail.com

Tweet@monaaeysha

Dr Mona

www.ingramcontent.com/pod-product-compliance
Lightning Source LLC
Chambersburg PA
CBHW070243290526
45789CB00004B/1742